From Doubt to Disciples: Unlocking the Great Commission

Andy Brown

Copyright © 2019 Andy Brown

All rights reserved.

ISBN: 9798280220942
ISBN-13: 9798280220942

CONTENTS

Foreword 5

Introduction 9

The Disciples' Dilemma: Bowing & Doubting 13

His Reign and our Response: "All Authority" 19

Beyond the Mountain: The Call to "Go!" 23

Becoming a Disciple Maker: Jesus' Instruction to "Make Disciples" 29

Waters of Grace: "Baptise Them" 37

The Command to Teach – Not Just For Pastors: "Teach Them" 45

The Promise of His Presence: "I Am With You" ... 51

To All Creation: "Mark's Take" 59

Don't Go! 71

About the Author 77

FOREWORD

I've read all sorts of books over the years. Some take very little effort. They are more akin to my eyes simply skipping along the words without taking them in. Others, to be honest, just defeated me! Because, sometimes - however good the author, or rich the content is - I can end up putting the book down simply because I just couldn't grasp what the author wanted me to see.

Andy Brown has a truly wonderful and refreshing approach to writing - about matters of the Bible; matters of the faith; matters of everyday life!

It's easy for me to read his books and, also, the posts he writes on his blog. They're easy to read not because they are either simple, or shallow. Actually, they are quite the opposite! And, yet, his approach opens the door to seeing issues we all face, only in a way that is easy to understand – which means you can enjoy just getting stuck into the text before you, getting just a little bit closer to Jesus with every word you absorb as you read.

The book ahead of you is worth your time and your investment. Andy explores matters of our Christian faith just deep enough to make you stop and think, while also finding yourself both comforted and encouraged. This is a style of writing to be both loudly celebrated and happily enjoyed. Because Andy also allows you to delve as deeply in the water of his writing as your mind is willing to wade – a rare gift in a book!

The Great Commission is the root and the source of our Christian faith; it is the very essence of everything and anything we do as Christians in our churches; in our families; in our workplace: it is the plumbline to all our actions as people.

We all need a key to open the door before us. But having a set of keys that can open multiple doors is always useful. This book is another key you'll be glad to have on your key ring.

Andy Berry

Andy B is the CEO of Pure247Radio.org and Editor at PureMediatheMagazine.com. He is also the founder of PureMediaFamily.com and one of the five original members at BerryBunch.org. He loves writing and inspiring others and is a Digital Missionary who 'lives by faith'.

He works, full-time, with his wife and their 3 sons in the North East of England. He is a natural kingdom builder who gets excited meeting others and encouraging them to always look up to Jesus Christ. He has been described as "a man with too many ideas" but his favourite things are really simple - walking in the countryside or enjoying a movie night with his family.

Find out more at his website
www.AndyBerry.co.uk
The Man - The Husband - The Father - The Son

Andy Brown

INTRODUCTION

In the early part of 2022, I felt compelled to write a short series on my blog about the Great Commission. It quickly evolved, and before I knew it, I had a first draft of this book completed. I am not a prolific writer by any stretch, but I often find when things come together so rapidly, it is often a sign that God is behind it.

My primary motivation for writing on this subject stemmed from what I perceived as a fundamental misunderstanding of its true nature. While many Christians are familiar with the term 'Great Commission,' the ability to readily articulate its components often eludes us. In the pages that follow, I aim to demonstrate that the Great Commission encompasses far more than simply sharing the message of Jesus.

My basic premise is that if we cannot describe the Commission left to us by Jesus, how can we ever hope to fulfil it?

This book endeavours to examine the Great Commission as presented in Matthew's Gospel, while also drawing insights from parallel accounts in Mark and Acts.

There are as many ways to fulfil this mission as there are people on the Earth. Each one of us will have a unique contribution and I cannot hope to set out the exact way you will respond. Instead, I plan to ask you a series of questions aimed at helping you think through the issue at hand, and come up with your own ideas about what you need to do.

The stereotypical view of an evangelist standing on a street corner handing out tracts may apply to you, but for many it will not. Your contribution to this mission will need to be God-inspired and Spirit-powered.

As you examine these commands (and they are commands) given to us by Jesus, ask yourself how you can personally fulfil them. Do not leave it to someone else, as they cannot do what you can.

While it may seem daunting, it is also exciting. Following Christ is no easy road, and you will face doubts and hardships. I do not say this to put you off, but want you to step into this with your eyes fully open. Daunting as it may be, there is nothing more important.

Your life on this world may only be for 70 or 80 years, but you can do things which will impact eternity.

How might God use you to increase His Kingdom? That is the question. Are you willing to explore the answer?

Andy Brown

Andy Brown

THE DISCIPLES' DILEMMA: BOWING & DOUBTING

Matthew's Gospel records the commands Jesus gave His disciples, commands that extend to us today.. The Great Commission' has become a well-known phrase within church circles, yet do we really know what it means?

If I asked you to sum up the Great Commission, what would you say? I wager that most would sum it up by saying "Telling others about Jesus!" This is true, in a broad sense, but the Great Commission is rather more specific than that.

Matthew's Gospel records the following:

> But the eleven disciples went into Galilee, to the mountain where Jesus had sent them. 17 When they saw him, they bowed down to him; but some doubted. 18 Jesus came to them and spoke to them, saying, "All authority has been given to me in heaven and on

> earth. 19 Go[b] and make disciples of all nations, baptizing them in the name of the Father and of the Son and of the Holy Spirit, 20 teaching them to observe all things that I commanded you. Behold, I am with you always, even to the end of the age." Amen.
>
> Matthew 28:16-20 (WEB)

After Jesus' death and resurrection, He makes an appointment with His disciples to meet Him in Galilee. Galilee, located in the north of Israel, required the disciples to journey upwards from Jerusalem.

Before we examine Jesus' words, let us first look at the important words leading up to them.

Verse 16 shows us that they went to Galilee, and then up the mountain as agreed. There, Jesus appears to them, and it records that they bow down. This, to me at least, implies that all eleven of them did indeed bow to the Risen Lord. They recognised not only the person of Jesus but also His now-revealed power and stature as the Risen Christ. This recognition of His divinity will be crucial when we examine Jesus' authority shortly.

Verse 17, however, contains a detail many

might overlook: 'but some doubted.' This revelation is striking This is not some large group barely familiar with Jesus, but the Eleven, the inner circle. For three years, they had walked alongside Jesus, witnessing His miracles of healing and resurrection. They had seen Him crucified, and now He stood before them, alive. And yet, some of them doubted

What this says to me is that faith and doubt are not mutually exclusive. We can have faith at the same time we are wrestling with doubt. Putting it another way, faith is not the absence of doubt, and nor is doubt the absence of faith.

We know that these men went on to die for their beliefs, some in horrendous ways, such as Peter, who was crucified upside down. Despite having "doubts," they did not allow them to hamper their faith.

The Eleven were not alone in their moments of doubt regarding Christ, both before and after His death. John the Baptist provides a significant example.

> Now when John heard in the prison the works of Christ, he sent two of his disciples 3 and said to him, "Are you he who comes, or should we look for another?"

Matthew 11:2-3 WEB

John, having prepared the way for Jesus, now finds himself in prison. He hears of the wonders that Christ is doing, and sends two disciples to ask, "Are you the One?" This contrasts sharply with his previous exclamation that Jesus is the Lamb of God (see John 1:29).

John had doubts it seems.

This is hardly surprising when you examine what happened to him. He was at the peak of his ministry, baptising in the Jordan and gathering many crowds. At the appearing of Jesus, things begin to change for him. Falling foul of the King, he ends up in prison. Lying in his prison cell at night, he likely gazed at the ceiling, questioning what had gone wrong. It is not a stretch to imagine him questioning whether Jesus was who he thought He was.

What did he do with that doubt? He took it

to Jesus.

This is a key point. When we doubt, and we all do at times, what do we do with it? I suppose in a broad sense, we have two choices. We either let those doubts take us away from Jesus, or we decide to take them to Him. John took his doubts to Christ. So did the Eleven.

As the Risen Lord stood before them, they bowed down and worshipped Him. Yet, at the same time, they had doubts. The Bible does not specifically say what the nature of their doubt was, but my suspicion is that it was to do with their view of who Jesus was.

Jesus did not remove the Roman rule, and did not free the people of Israel from their subjection from earthly authority – as everyone had hoped and expected. Even now, in His risen glory, He does not do it!

The freedom that Christ brought in His first appearing was not from Roman rule, but from sin's clutches. That is the message He wants us to take to the world.

For us, I think the lesson is that it is ok to have questions. There is much we do not understand, and it is simply not possible to have all the answers before we commit to Jesus. We should take our questions to the Lord and prayerfully seek the answers.

If we allow it, our doubt can drag us away from God. Let us learn the lessons from both John the Baptist and the Eleven disciples. Jesus is more than capable of handling our doubts and fears.

What will you do?

At the end of each chapter in this book, I will ask you this question: what will you do in response to what you have read?

As we consider bowing and doubting, I ask:

- When you struggle with doubt, do you let it bring you closer or further from God?
- What steps can you take to relieve a particular doubt you have?
- Is there a trusted and wise friend you can talk to about some questions you have?

HIS REIGN AND OUR RESPONSE: "ALL AUTHORITY"

> Jesus came to them and spoke to them, saying, "All authority has been given to me in heaven and on earth.
>
> Matthew 28:18 (WEB)

Before we examine Jesus' commission to us in the coming chapters, we must first understand (and accept) His authority. Here, He states quite clearly that all authority in heaven and on earth has been given to Him. That means, simply put, He is in charge.

Jesus does not offer guidance, nor advice, nor encouragement. Instead, He sets out His total authority over all things and then tells us what to do, making it clear that this is not optional and cannot be ignored..

Consider if you went to court and the judge ordered you to do something. It is not optional for you, but the authority of the court now compels you to follow its instructions. To not comply could lead to hefty fines or worse, incarceration.

You cannot ask yourself if you feel like doing whatever it is the court asks of you. You cannot offer excuses. You cannot put it off nor get someone else to do it for you. You *must* do what the court has ordered.

When Jesus gives us these commands, He expects them to be followed and He is backed by all authority under heaven. Do we treat His words accordingly?

I recall an incident at work several years ago where I, the manager of an individual, instructed them to do something. It was a reasonable thing for me to ask, yet it went undone. When I asked the person about it, they told me that it was not something they liked to do, and so just did not bother.

How do you think that went? Do you think I replied by saying, "Oh that's fine, I'm sorry to put you out. In fact, let me do it for you!" Assuredly not! Instead, I restated my instruction and warned them of the consequences of not fulfilling the requirements of their job.

We may offer Jesus excuses, telling Him we are afraid, embarrassed, or that we simply do not have the time. However, He will not change His mind. He will, again, give us those very same commands.

The point I want to make, as we begin this study together, is for us to understand that Jesus sets out His authority because He expects us to do what He says. We will look at what is involved in this in the coming chapters, but let us begin by submitting to His authority, and deciding in our hearts that we will do whatever it is He is about to ask us.

Jesus is our Saviour. He has rescued us from the power of sin, and we cannot doubt His loving kindness and care towards us. He is also our Lord too, our King even. He may be closer than a brother, but let us not forget who is really in charge.

What will you do?

Consider these questions:

- If you bow down to Christ as Lord, do you feel compelled to do what He has asked of you?
- Are you prepared to fully submit yourself to Jesus' authority, and act accordingly? Be honest, and take the answer to God in prayer.
- Why do we find submission difficult?

Andy Brown

BEYOND THE MOUNTAIN: THE CALL TO "GO!"

> Jesus came to them and spoke to them, saying, "All authority has been given to me in heaven and on earth. 19 Go and make disciples of all nations, baptizing them in the name of the Father and of the Son and of the Holy Spirit, 20 teaching them to observe all things that I commanded you. Behold, I am with you always, even to the end of the age." Amen.
>
> Matthew 28:18-20 WEB

Having established His authority, the Lord Jesus begins to command His Eleven disciples. Jesus is neither vague, nor unclear. He sets out for them several things they must now go and do to fulfil this Great Commission, and we will examine each in turn in the proceeding chapters.

Every journey must begin with the very first step. For the Great Commission, the first step is to simply "Go!"

To go is an action. It is not standing still and letting the world pass you by, but it is to move, and move forwards.

The Eleven would never fulfil this mission if they had set up camp on that mountainside. Had they stayed there, discussing what Jesus had told them or all the things that had happened, then we may never have heard of them again. Had they formed a committee to decide the best course of action, taking a vote on the right direction to travel in or what was the best approach to teaching, then they would have been paralysed on the spot.

There is a place for discussion, planning and committees, don't get me wrong, but there is also a time for action. I do not advise you to jump into something without prior thought, but neither do I suggest you sit around shooting the breeze.

Go! Says the Lord, move out and together we will change the world.

It does not matter how far you go, as long as you do go. Whether you walk a dozen steps to your neighbour's house, travel half a mile to the local town square, or cross the globe to a far-flung nation, go and take the message of Christ with you.

Using a Bible search engine, the word "Go" appears over 1400 times in the KJV version of the Scriptures, whereas the word "stop" only occurs 7 times! Clearly God wants us to get the message that we are to go, pressing on and doing the work He has called us to. Ask yourself, "Do I more often "stop" or "go?"

Philip was told "Go!" and he went to Samaria:

> Philip went down to the city of Samaria, and proclaimed to them the Christ. 6 The multitudes listened with one accord to the things that were spoken by Philip when they heard and saw the signs which he did. 7 For unclean spirits came out of many of those who had them. They came out, crying with a loud voice. Many who had been paralyzed and lame were healed. 8 There was great joy in that city.
>
> Acts 8:5-8 WEB

Paul followed the command to go, and he went to the Gentiles, Peter did likewise, but to the Jewish people:

> Then after a period of fourteen years I went up again to Jerusalem with Barnabas, taking Titus also with me. 2 I went up by revelation, and I laid before them the Good News which I preach among the Gentiles, but privately before those who were respected, for fear that I might be running, or had run, in vain.
> but to the contrary, when they saw that I had been entrusted with the Good News for the uncircumcised, even as Peter with the Good News for the circumcised— 8 for he who worked through Peter in the apostleship with the circumcised also worked through me with the Gentiles
>
> Galatians 2:1-2, 7-8 WEB

Moses was told to go to Pharoah. Jonah was instructed to go to Nineveh. God told Joshua to go and conquer the land. Elijah told the widow of Zarephath to go, and bring him a cake, and she went, receiving a miracle. Likewise, Elisha told another widow to go and get empty jars that they might be filled with oil, and she, too, went.

Where is God telling you to go?

The Point of this chapter is not some deep theological diatribe (nice word!), but rather to encourage and inspire you. I am not revealing some great doctrinal truth, but instead am directing you to action. We will never fulfil the Great Commission without it.

For you to go may mean a shift in your attitude, habits or thinking. It may not mean a change in physical location, but a definite decision to alter your mindset and do whatever Christ is calling you to.

When you go, you may need to leave certain "baggage" behind you. Gossiping friends, TV addiction, the comfort of familiarity or just plain old worries may need to be discarded so you can fully go for the Lord.

The word "go" means to move or proceed, as I think I have emphasised above. It can also mean to start or begin, as in to fire the starting gun on the racetrack.

This exclamation – Go! – is a trigger for us to begin. When that starting gun fires, the runners do not amble along, enjoying the sunshine and having a chat! No, they leap forward with energy and vigour, and that is precisely how we ought to launch into the Great Commission.

I do not want you to proceed without haste; to just quit your job, up sticks and charge ahead without clear direction from God. That is not wise. I do want you to proceed with urgency, energy and excitement however, giving this all you have.

Make a firm decision today that you are going to follow Christ and all He commands with everything you have. Join me, and let's go!

What will you do?

My questions to you today are:

- What does it mean for you to "go?"
- Is there anything hindering you, or holding you back from going?
- Can you think of anyone else from the Bible who was told to go, and what can you learn from them?

BECOMING A DISCIPLE MAKER: JESUS' INSTRUCTION TO "MAKE DISCIPLES"

> Jesus came to them and spoke to them, saying, "All authority has been given to me in heaven and on earth. 19 Go and make disciples of all nations, baptizing them in the name of the Father and of the Son and of the Holy Spirit, 20 teaching them to observe all things that I commanded you. Behold, I am with you always, even to the end of the age." Amen.
>
> Matthew 28:18-20 WEB

In the full power of His authority, Jesus tells His disciples to go. Giving specifics now, He instructs them to complete three primary tasks – the first of these being to make disciples. In subsequent chapters, we will look at the other two instructions which are to baptise and to teach.

Firstly, what is a disciple? We cannot hope to "make" them if we are not clear what they are.

A disciple is simply a "follower." A disciple of Jesus, therefore, is one who follows Him.

Following someone is most commonly used in physical terms. We follow someone when they are showing us the right way to go. Perhaps you are going to a new place and you do not know the way, if you follow a friend then they go on ahead and you tag along behind.

We can follow in many more ways than just physical, however. You may, for example, follow your favourite sports teams; keeping up with their scores, team news and key stats. Likewise, you might follow a singer or band, streaming their latest music and "following" them on the socials.

To follow Christ means something rather deeper. It implies a firm commitment to Him, and not to be a mere "fan" of His, but instead to devote your life in His service. Following Jesus is to follow in His footsteps, and again, I do not mean physically. We aspire to be more and more like Him; walking in love, being unselfish, caring for others, but most importantly, bringing people into a deeper relationship with the Father.

To be Christ's disciple is to put aside all else, and follow Him with your whole heart.

We learn about Him yes, but we learn with Him. We do what He asks of us, and we put Him first above all else. We follow Jesus into blessing, and we follow Him into troubles and trials. We sacrifice what this world has to offer and instead choose His glory. We put our trust in Him, relying on Him for our life in this world and the next. That is what it is to be a disciple.

So how do we "make" them?

Earlier on, I asked how you would sum up the Great Commission, and pointed out that many might answer by saying "Telling others about Jesus." Sharing the Good News about Christ is the first step to making disciples.

> For, "Whoever will call on the name of the Lord will be saved." 14 How then will they call on him in whom they have not believed? How will they believe in him whom they have not heard? How will they hear without a

> preacher? 15 And how will they preach unless they are sent? As it is written: "How beautiful are the feet of those who preach the Good News of peace,
>   who bring glad tidings of good things!"
>
> Romans 10:13-15 WEB

They cannot call on the name of the Lord and begin to follow Him unless they are first told. To begin making disciples, we must tell them the truth. We tell them the Gospel, which is that Christ came, He lived and died, and on the third day He rose again to new life. Whoever believes in Him will live and have eternal life! Praise His Holy Name!

Is telling those who do not know Jesus enough to make disciples? For some it might be. They hear the word preached to them, and the Spirit of God stirs up their hearts to make a lifelong commitment to Him. For others, they may start to accept and believe the truth of the Gospel, but will then need love, support and guidance. For all of us, there is a substantial journey between the moment we give our lives to Jesus, and the time we reach maturity in the faith.

This is why God has given the church a variety of gifts and offices:

> He gave some to be apostles; and some, prophets; and some, evangelists; and some, shepherds and teachers;
>
> Ephesians 4:11 (WEB)

In this text, Paul sets out five "offices" of the church. Each serves a unique purpose in making disciples. This book is perhaps not the right place to explore each of these designated offices in detail. Needless to say though, each specific role comes to together in unity to bring about God's will and purpose.

Our goal in making disciples is not simply to get someone to mouth the words "I believe in Jesus," but rather we want them to experience the changed life that comes from being a true follower of Christ. At times we need to be taught the truth, and at other times we need the care of the shepherd or pastor. There are times we may need the warning or encouragement of the prophet, and many begin our journeys responding to the call of the evangelist. All are involved in making disciples.

All Nations

Carefully reading Jesus' words again shows us that "make disciples" is not the full command, instead He tells us to "make disciples of all nations." This shows us that no one is excluded. God wants His Gospel preached everywhere, and to have disciples present in all places. You might consider the collective disciples as the global church, which is God's hands and feet, reaching every corner of the globe.

No one person can do this. If you are worried you might have to travel far and wide to begin making disciples, then let me reassure you. There are plenty of opportunities on your doorstep. Perhaps God may call some of us to go to far off places and make disciples there, but for the most part we are to do it in our own backyard.

We can make disciples in our own family. We can make disciples of our work friends. We can make disciples of our neighbours. We can make disciples of our followers on social. And if we write, we can make disciples of Christ of our readers.

One of the great things about writing a blog (and you can find mine at andy-brown.org) is that the stats tell you where your readers come from. I live in the UK, and many of my readers come from there, but I also see readers from places I am never likely to go. It is humbling that my words, such as they are, reach such places. It remains my continued prayer that those who do read will become more and more like Christ. That is, surely, what making disciples is all about.

What will you do?

Some questions for you to think about:

- How well are you following Jesus?
- What is your role in making disciples, do you think?
- Can you think of someone who may need encouraging in their walk with Jesus today?

Andy Brown

WATERS OF GRACE: "BAPTISE THEM"

> Jesus came to them and spoke to them, saying, "All authority has been given to me in heaven and on earth. 19 Go and make disciples of all nations, baptizing them in the name of the Father and of the Son and of the Holy Spirit, 20 teaching them to observe all things that I commanded you. Behold, I am with you always, even to the end of the age." Amen.
>
> Matthew 28:18-20 (WEB)

Jesus gave three primary instructions to His eleven followers on the mountain.

1. Make disciples of all nations

2. Baptise them in the name of the Father, Son and Holy Spirit

3. Teach them to obey all He commanded

We now consider number two on the list, namely the instruction to baptise.

In some respects, I feel this is a forgotten element of the Great Commission. I have said previously that simply telling others about Jesus is not quite enough to fulfil the task at hand, and this particular instruction is relevant. Telling others about Christ and the Gospel does not equate to baptism.

We must not neglect the command of baptism in the Great Commission.

For the individual, this may feel somewhat difficult to fulfil. It is clear that we ought not to run around throwing holy water on people, baptising them with a super-soaker! For the most part, we tend to leave this instruction to be fulfilled by the church, rather than us as members of it.

While the act of baptising is typically carried out within the church community by those appointed to do so, individual believers have a vital role to play in supporting this significant step. We can encourage those who are exploring faith or have recently come to believe to consider baptism as a natural and important act of obedience. Sharing our own experiences of baptism, where appropriate, can be a powerful testimony. Furthermore, we can offer practical support to those preparing for baptism, such as praying for them, celebrating with them, and welcoming them fully into the fellowship of the church. Our enthusiasm and support can help to underscore the importance and joy of this public declaration of faith, making it a truly meaningful experience for all involved.

To be clear, baptism is a symbolic event where water is used to indicate the new life of a believer seeking to follow Christ. It is a public declaration of an internal change. When we surrender ourselves to Jesus, He gives us a heart of flesh instead of stone, and gifts us with His Holy Spirit to dwell with us. Baptism, then, is an outward sign of that commitment.

Baptism is more than just a symbol however; it carries profound theological weight. In the baptismal waters, we find a powerful echo of Christ's own death and resurrection. Just as He was buried and rose to new life, so too, through baptism, the believer identifies with this pivotal act. It signifies the death of our old life, the washing away of sin, and our being raised with Christ to walk in newness of life. Furthermore, baptism marks our entrance into the family of God, publicly declaring our allegiance to Christ and uniting us with the community of believers. It is the first step of obedience in our new life, a tangible expression of the inward transformation that has taken place through faith.

Different church traditions do this in a variety of ways. Some will completely immerse an individual in water, using a pool or even the ocean. Others simply sprinkle water over them as a symbol of cleansing. Some church traditions baptise children or infants, while others only adults.

On that last point, it is clear that as an infant, you cannot make the promises required for a real commitment for Christ. Instead, it is the parents and godparents who make those promises on the child's behalf, and later in life it is hoped the child will make the promises for themselves. In the Anglican tradition, a baptised infant, when they reach an age of understanding, can then go forward for "Confirmation" which is essentially adopting the baptismal promises for themselves.

Whatever your tradition, and whatever your views on infant baptism or total immersion, the command from Jesus is clear – we are to baptise.

A friend of mine came to faith in his twenties, but was never baptised. He had not been baptised as a baby, and his church had not emphasised the need for it. When he moved home and thus changed to a different fellowship, he became involved in serving at the church. One day when the pastor was teaching on the subject of baptism, he came to the decision that he must be baptised as a sign of his belief.

Did it enhance his faith in any particular way? Was he not "properly" saved until he was immersed? Was it just a good excuse for a get-together? The likely answer is no to all of these (although some may disagree) but the point is it was a definite step of obedience. Baptism is a command of Christ, and this man fulfilled it.

As he climbed down the steps into the water, it represented the death and burial of his old life of sin. As he emerged from the surface of the water, it depicted his freshness as a "new creation" in Christ. This is what baptism is all about.

The Father, Son and Holy Spirit

Jesus instructs His followers to baptise in the Name of the Father, Son and Holy Spirit. To be honest, there is some debate about this point. Are these not titles, rather than names? Some will ask. Is it not sufficient to baptise in the "name" of Jesus?

There is something a rabbit hole to avoid here. The issue is not unimportant of course, and I urge you to investigate it for yourself. We do not have time in these brief words to give the topic justice.

The critical point for me here is that we are not baptised into any old name. We are not pinning our colours to any random mast. Instead, we are dedicating ourselves to the Triune God – Father, Son and Holy Spirit. This is the God of Abraham, Isaac and Jacob. He is the God of the Bible, and the One who raised Christ from the dead. You cannot easily separate the Father from the Son, nor the Spirit from Jesus. They are One God, in three Persons. To fully understand this is to comprehend God Himself, which is beyond any of us.

How we baptise is a matter for study and debate, and various church traditions have grown up over time with differing views. The point is we *are* to baptise.

Having gone out, as Jesus told us, and sharing the Good News about Christ, a natural step for those who believe is to be baptised. For many people, it is a key event in their lives of faith. Often it marks the beginning of something too.

Jesus was baptised by John in the River Jordan, which you can read about in Matthew 3. This was not to cleanse Jesus from sin, as He was without it, but instead marked the coming of the Spirit and the beginning of His earthly ministry.

In a similar way, perhaps you need to experience baptism for yourself, or renew the promises you or other made for you?

What will you do?

Some questions for you today:

- Have you been baptised, and if not, does this encourage you to explore it?

- Does your church teach about baptism and encourage it?
- If you were baptised as a child, why not review the promises that were made on your behalf today, and commit yourself to keeping them?

THE COMMAND TO TEACH – NOT JUST FOR PASTORS: "TEACH THEM"

> Jesus came to them and spoke to them, saying, "All authority has been given to me in heaven and on earth. 19 Go and make disciples of all nations, baptizing them in the name of the Father and of the Son and of the Holy Spirit, 20 teaching them to observe all things that I commanded you. Behold, I am with you always, even to the end of the age." Amen.
>
> Matthew 28:18-20 (WEB)

The substance of our Christian lives ought to be different from that of the world. If we talk the same, act the same, think the same, and do all the same things that the world does, then we must question whether we are truly born anew. Disciples are not meant to be the "same" as those who follow their own fleshy or sinful desires.

If that is a shock to you, then perhaps the Great Commission has yet to be fulfilled in your life. Maybe you have believed in Christ, accepting Him as Lord and Saviour, yet no one has taken the time to teach you to obey.

And so, we come to the third part of the Great Commission which Jesus gave to us. To teach disciples all that He commanded.

Obedience may not seem like a very exciting topic to you, yet it is crucial we learn to observe what Jesus told us to do. It will lead us to God's kind of success, blessing and most importantly, the glory of God.

Having made disciples, and baptising them in the name of the Father, Son and Spirit, we must then teach them. This task will take a lifetime, and most people (myself definitely included) are slow learners!

Where do we begin? I suspect there is no right or wrong answer to this, and it might be different for everyone.

Firstly, we are to teach people to obey all that Jesus commanded. We might strictly interpret this to mean following only the red letters in our Bible, and thus dismissing most of the epistles and the entirety of the Old Testament… I do not think this is so however!

> Every Scripture is God-breathed and[a] profitable for teaching, for reproof, for correction, and for instruction in righteousness,
>
> 2 Timothy 3:16 (WEB)

The entirety of Scripture, the totality of God's Word in both the Old and New Testaments, the letters, the history and the prophecy are all inspired by the Spirit of Christ. In my opinion, it is all to be taught and learned.

Now can you see why it might take a lifetime?

How can we teach the entirety of the Bible ourselves? Again, I believe it is a team effort. If you are a pastor, or are called to teach, then it might be more obvious how you can fulfil this part of the Great Commission. Use your pulpit, wherever it is, and teach the people to obey Christ. You may lead a church or be privileged to speak at one, you may write a blog or books, or you may be recording and sharing videos on YouTube or other media platforms. All of that contributes to the teaching of God's people.

For the rest though, who do not have such platforms, or who do not feel called to teach, how can they comply with Christ's instruction to teach?

Parents can and should teach their children. Older members of the church family may instruct the younger. The members of a small group will encourage and challenge one another, whether they are leading the discussion or just participating. As we do life together, the church ought to be helping each other to grow in faith and obedience.

Even if you personally have little opportunity to teach someone with your words, let your actions be the lesson.

> Be imitators of me, even as I also am of Christ.
>
> 1 Corinthians 11:1 (WEB)

Here, the apostle Paul, urges the Corinthian church to follow him, as he follows Jesus. Imitate me, he cries, as I imitate Christ. This is not easy, and if we take a hard look at ourselves, we may not feel like the best examples of Jesus' lifestyle. But each of us should be striving forward to observe what

Christ has taught us, and as we do, let us bring others along for the ride.

Sometimes we think of the Great Commission as only relating to evangelism. I hope these words have shown you that it is not so. Fulfilling this Commission does, of course, involve telling others about our faith, but it also encapsulates our journey into maturity as believers. I do not think there is one Christian who can claim to observe all that Jesus commanded us, and so we are all to keep walking with Him, bearing fruit and growing in faith.

What can you do?

I want to ask you:

- How well do you feel you obeying Jesus at the moment?
- What is your "pulpit"? i.e. in what ways can you be a teacher and encourage others to obey Christ?
- What one thing can you do to be a better example for Jesus?

- Consider your own journey of faith; who has been instrumental in teaching you to obey Christ? How can you do the same for someone else?

THE PROMISE OF HIS PRESENCE: "I AM WITH YOU"

> Jesus came to them and spoke to them, saying, "All authority has been given to me in heaven and on earth. 19 Go and make disciples of all nations, baptizing them in the name of the Father and of the Son and of the Holy Spirit, 20 teaching them to observe all things that I commanded you. Behold, I am with you always, even to the end of the age." Amen.
>
> Matthew 28:18-20 (WEB)

Over the course of this book, we have examined the Great Commission found in Matthew's Gospel. I hope these words have further illuminated the Commission, and that it goes beyond simply sharing our faith – although that is clearly part of it.

In summary, Jesus tells His Eleven - and by extension, us as well – that they are to go, to make disciples, to baptise and to teach people to obey Him. We have explored each of these in turn, and I now ask you to reflect on how you can contribute to fulfilling each element.

I am sure you agree that this is no small task! If you are feeling a little daunted by the idea of trying to fulfil this Commission, then you are not alone.

Jesus' promise to remain with us until the end of the age is no platitude. He really is "with you." That means fulfilling the Great Commission is achievable because of His presence beside us.

The first thing to remember is that God will never ask you to do anything that you cannot do. He would be unjust to do so. God's nature is one of love and understanding; He does not delight in our struggles.. Instead, God never lets us go through things we cannot bear.

> No temptation has taken you except what is common to man. God is faithful, who will not allow you to be tempted above what you are able, but will with the temptation also make the

> way of escape, that you may be able to endure it.
>
> 1 Corinthians 10:13 (WEB)

Paul, talking of temptation here, points out that God does not allow any temptation beyond that which we can bear. He will provide a way of escape so that no temptation will overcome us.

In a similar way, I believe God will not lay a command us on that we cannot complete. He equips us with all we need to succeed, be it gifts, talents, resources or indeed His very own Spirit.

That is not to say He will not ask us to do difficult things. Part of our spiritual growth and maturity is developing our ability to suffer under trial. Why? So we learn to more deeply rely on God, and point others to do the same when they face times of testing.

It is also important to remember that we are not expected to fulfil this task all on our own. We may have individual responsibilities yes, but it is not on any one person to complete this great work solo. We work together, as a family of believers, and united as the Church of God, we can complete the mission before us.

> For as the body is one, and has many members, and all the members of the body, being many, are one body; so also, is Christ. 13 For in one Spirit we were all baptized into one body, whether Jews or Greeks, whether bond or free; and were all given to drink into one Spirit. 14 For the body is not one member, but many.
>
> 1 Corinthians 12:12-14 (WEB)

We, the church, are one body. We are made up of different parts, but all exist together as one, and only by co-operating can we hope to fulfil the Great Commission. I may be able to write (to some extent) but I surely cannot sing! What if someone is to be reached with a tuneful rendition of a biblical song? You will not be able to call on me to do this! Instead, you will need a different part of the body.

The truth is that you cannot do everything, but you can do something. God has purposely made us all different, and so each of us can bring our unique gifts, talents and experiences to bear. I cannot do it all, and neither can you, but together we can do significantly more.

Jesus commitment to us as individuals is matched by His commitment to His Bride – the Church. He promises to be with us, and reiterates this by saying "where two or three are gathered… there I will be." (my paraphrase. It is not a personal promise as much as it is a corporate one.

I Am With You

> Behold, I am with you always, even to the end of the age." Amen.

Matthew 28:20b

Not only do we have one another's help and support, we have Jesus' too. Here, He tells us plainly that He is with us and will remain that way.

When we "go" in faith, stepping out to make disciples, baptise and teach, we do so with the Lord Himself. One of the keys to success is not trying to do this in our own strength, but in His. No one comes to the Father except through Christ Himself (John 14:6) so attempting to do this without Him is fruitless.

I recall a time when my wife and I had to move some furniture in our home. One of our children, who were rather young at the time, tried to help us. Their little amount of strength was insufficient to move the item, but with their father's help, the job was completed.

Trying to fulfil the Great Commission without the strength and power of the Lord is like a little child trying to pick up and move a bed. It cannot be done.

I am reminded of Jesus' words from earlier in Matthew's Gospel:

> Take my yoke upon you and learn from me, for I am gentle and humble in heart; and you will find rest for your souls.
>
> Matthew 11:29 (WEB)

A yoke combines the power of two or more oxen, so that the plough is more easily moved, and the work done. If you only put one ox in the yoke, it will be lopsided and likely move in circles. Jesus asks us to unite with Him, and together the task will be completed.

Do not go it alone, but go out with Christ. He has promised to be with you, and only by working with Him can you extend His kingdom and share the Good News with the world. It is a great mystery that God chooses to involve us in His plans, yet I rejoice in that mystery and in being a part of that family.

I leave you with this thought; in heaven, you will be able to pray, to worship, to study Scripture, to fellowship with God and His people, but the one thing you cannot do is fulfil the Great Commission. Let this spur you on, united with the church, and in the power of the Spirit. Let us go out, make disciples, baptise and teach, knowing that Jesus is with us. Amen!

What will you do?

Ask yourselves these questions today:

- What comfort do you gain from knowing Christ is with you?
- How can you practically draw on His strength more?
- Having read this book, what three things can you do now to participate in this great mission?

Andy Brown

TO ALL CREATION: "MARK'S TAKE"

> He said to them, "Go into all the world, and preach the Good News to the whole creation. 16 He who believes and is baptized will be saved; but he who disbelieves will be condemned. 17 These signs will accompany those who believe: in my name they will cast out demons; they will speak with new languages; 18 they will take up serpents; and if they drink any deadly thing, it will in no way hurt them; they will lay hands on the sick, and they will recover."
>
> Mark 16:15-18 (WEB)

Matthew's Gospel is not the only place where the Great Commission is recorded. There is some debate about whether Mark's verses above are the very same account Matthew describes, or rather a variation on a theme from a different episode. Some even question whether the above was in Mark's original manuscript at all.

Leaving all of that to one side, there is great value in examining these words. What more do we learn about our mission given to us by Jesus? Does it add or enhance what we have already learned from Matthew's account?

Preach to All Creation

Verse 15 restates the command to go, adding that we are to preach to "all creation." Some translations render this as "to all creatures." Some have taken this literally and even preach to the animal or plant kingdom.

St Anthony of Padua visited a town and preached the Gospel. It seems he got little response and so went down to the riverbank. It is said that he preached right there, and the fish of the river came and schooled around him. The people of the village were so convicted that the animals would listen where they would not, that they came to hear the Good News.

I cannot tell you how true this is, and will leave you to make up your own mind. It raises the question though, should we preach to *all* creation?

My view is simply no. Sorry if that disappoints you! And I am not suggesting you somehow ignore Christ's commands here. Instead, although this word (in the Greek) can mean creation, or the "sum of creation" it can also simply mean "created being." While the creation is as much stained by sin as humanity is, there is no evidence from Scripture that we are to preach to animals or plants. Even if you can argue that point, you must concede that our focus ought to be on humanity first, and there are plenty of those who need to hear the Good News before we turn our attention elsewhere!

More on Baptism

Verse 16 again sounds familiar to us who have studied Matthew's account. Jesus tells us plainly that whoever believes and is baptised, will be saved. Those who disbelieve as condemned.

Notice the more direct pronoun here. The word "he" is far more personal than "they". Matthew says, "baptise them," whereas Mark (the more direct of the Gospels) say "he who believes and is baptised." "Them" may refer to someone else, that is, someone other than us. But "he" refers to the one; you or I.

Like Matthew, the implication here is that baptism is a requirement. The text says whoever "believes *and* is baptised." In and of itself, you might rightly ask if simply believing is enough?

I have pondered this point, and as I wrote in the earlier chapter "Baptise Them." I framed baptism as something we are commanded to do, but not necessarily as something which saved us. Baptism without belief clearly does not save.

Notice Jesus' contrasting point here, that he who does not believe is condemned. There is no mention of baptism. Why? Simply because if you do not believe there would be no reason for you to be baptised at all.

So, must we both believe and be baptised to be saved? Some will tell you yes, and I urge you to investigate the matter for yourself. Do not simply take my word for it.

It is my view that belief must always be followed by corresponding action. James, in his letter, points out that believing is all well and good, but even the demons *believe*! Belief that results in no corresponding action is worthless.

If we believe, then we ought to do what Jesus tells us to do – namely, to be baptised.

There are passages in the Bible which we could examine to look at both sides of this argument. As I say above, do search out the Scriptures yourself for the truth. I want to remind you of the criminal crucified with Christ though.

> He said to Jesus, "Lord, remember me when you come into your Kingdom."
>
> 43 Jesus said to him, "Assuredly I tell you, today you will be with me in Paradise."
>
> Luke 23:42-43 (WEB)

Here, the robber who had earlier hurled insults on Christ, essentially makes a confession of faith. He does not ask for forgiveness, nor pray the "Sinner's Prayer," but he finally looks to the Lord as he faces his death.

Jesus does not deny him, nor points to his lack of baptism. Instead, Christ assures him that he, too, will join Jesus in paradise.

This robber had little opportunity to join his faith with action, but was apparently not excluded because of it.

I know that some will argue for or against this passage as proof or otherwise. I submit it to you and hope you have not interpreted my words as telling anyone not to be baptised. IF you believe in Jesus, and if you have not been baptised, then go and make that public declaration of your faith. Speak to your church leadership about it, and celebrate your salvation.

Signs Following

> These signs will accompany those who believe: in my name they will cast out demons; they will speak with new languages; 18 they will take up serpents; and if they drink any deadly thing, it will in no way hurt them; they will lay hands on the sick, and they will recover."

Mark 16:17-18 (WEB)

Verses 17 and 18 add something of a new dimension to the Great Commission. Jesus, in Matthew, set out what we are to, and Mark reiterates the key points for us. Mark then adds these rather challenging words.

"These signs *will* accompany them who believe…" verse 17 says, with my emphasis added. It does not say *may* or *might*. Are we to take this as expectation?

It is interesting that, in my experience, some are very strict on the interpretation of, for example, verse 16 and insist baptism is a requirement of salvation (I touched on this above) and yet are far less strict on these verses about signs. What I mean is, they might insist on baptism for salvation, but do not insist on signs, wonders and miracles following those that preach the Gospel.

Some go to extremes in the other direction though, demanding signs and wonders to be present with the preaching of the Good News, otherwise it "does not count."

In an attempt to take the text seriously, and yet being balanced, it does not say such things must happen every single time we preach. So, if there is no healing at your church service this coming Sunday, that does not make your pastor a false teacher!

These words of Christ should challenge us though. Having said I do not think these signs are a mandatory element of all church gatherings, I also do not think we should ignore or forget about them. We must not chase after them, but neither should we fail to expect them. Too few are open to the possibility of God intervening in some miraculous way.

If we truly believe, and if we are preaching the full counsel of God, then we must be open to the possibility of such wonders occurring in our midst. More than that, we should have an expectation of them.

Miracles are not meant to be "normal." If they were an everyday occurrence, then they would cease to be miracles and instead just be daily life. That is quite a step away from never expecting them however, and I believe we ought to be open to how God wants to do things.

The signs that are listed here are:

- Casting out demons
- Speaking in new languages
- Being unharmed by deadly serpents
- Being unharmed by deadly poisons

- The healing of the sick

Please notice it does not say we should go and find deadly snakes and drink deadly poisons. Likewise, we are not instructed to go "demon-hunting" either. These signs are given to us in the context of fulfilling the Great Commission. Should we, in the course of our Gospel preaching, encounter such things, then we have the authority to deal with them.

It is not my intention to delve further into these wonders in this little book. It would all too easy to enter into various controversies about speaking in tongues or the reasons why we do not always see or receive healing. That is not the point of this work.

Mark's take on the Great Commission offers us additional tools we can deploy for the success of the Gospel. He does not intend for us to be some kind of Christian superhero, with mighty powers and a cape! Rather, the glory should always belong to the Lord.

As we preach and share the Good News, such signs follow us as a way of authenticating the words we use.

The most powerful of all the tools in our arsenal is the Bible itself. No one is born anew in God without the heart changing power of the Scriptures.

Peter says:

> Seeing you have purified your souls in your obedience to the truth through the Spirit in sincere brotherly affection, love one another from the heart fervently, 23 having been born again, not of corruptible seed, but of incorruptible, through the word of God, which lives and remains forever.

1 peter 1:22-23 WEB

We are born again by the incorruptible seed, which Peter shows us is the Word of God. Signs, miracles and wonders may attract attention, but they do not save.

Let each of us preach the Gospel to all creation, and as we do, may such signs follow us, but let us never forget it is the truth of the Bible which sets humanity free.

What will you do?

Think about these questions:

- What does Mark's account add to the Great Commission?
- How might you be more open to signs following the preaching of the Gospel (remembering to be led first and foremost by the Bible)?
- What other Scriptures or resources might you use to help understand the relationship between believing, baptism and salvation?

Andy Brown

DON'T GO!

Being assembled together with them, he commanded them, "Don't depart from Jerusalem, but wait for the promise of the Father, which you heard from me. 5 For John indeed baptized in water, but you will be baptized in the Holy Spirit not many days from now."
6 Therefore when they had come together, they asked him, "Lord, are you now restoring the kingdom to Israel?"

7 He said to them, "It isn't for you to know times or seasons which the Father has set within his own authority. 8 But you will receive power when the Holy Spirit has come upon you. You will be witnesses to me in Jerusalem, in all Judea and Samaria, and to the uttermost parts of the

earth."

Acts 1:4-8 (WEB)

Don't go? Surely that is a direct contradiction to what I told you in an earlier chapter?
True, although technically the above says "Don't depart…" not "Don't go!"

This does, on the surface, seem like Matthew 28 is telling us to go, and yet Jesus (here in Acts) is saying wait. Wait for what? For the promise of the Holy Spirit.

So, it is not "Don't go…" But rather, "Don't go… without the Spirit's help."

It is helpful to understand the timeline here. If you are to look at the chronology, then it is likely that Matthew 28 (and also Mark 16) occurs prior to Acts 1. After Jesus' death in Jerusalem, the disciples travel north to Galilee to meet Him on the mountain. There, they receive the Great Commission and after travel back to Jerusalem.

In Jerusalem, the Lord appears to them again and gives them the commands we have read in Acts 1.

So, in a sense, Matthew 28 is a general instruction for what they will go on to do. In Acts, Jesus tells them not to begin to try and fulfil Matthew 28 without first having received the gift of the Spirit.

As we draw near to the end of this book, it is very important you understand this point. You cannot complete this mission without God's help. You need the power and presence of the Holy Spirit in order to be Christ's witnesses in the world.

Preaching the Gospel, making disciples, teaching, preparing people for baptism; these are all elements of the Great Commission, and all require God's power in and through us to make it happen.

If we attempt this on our own, without God's help, we will struggle and fail. We (humans) cannot convict people of their sin and convince them of their need for a Saviour, we need the Spirit of Jesus to do this.

My words, whether in print or in person, lack power without the anointing of God. Yours do too, I wager.

Misunderstood

Verses 6 and 7 of Acts 1 describe the disciples asking Jesus if He will now restore the kingdom to Israel. Still, they do not understand.

They lived and worked with Him for three years during His ministry. They watched Him die on a cross. They saw Him, alive again, on the mountain in Galilee (among other places). They see Him again now in their very midst. Yet, He remains misunderstood.

One day, Jesus will return and take His rightful place as King. The disciples thought, believed and expected Him to do it both before and after His death. Even in the passage above, their expectation is growing, as is their excitement, as He speaks of the power that will be bestowed upon them.

Perhaps they imagine they will become mighty warriors, and that this gifted power will enable them to fight the Romans and kick them out. They misunderstood.

Jesus rebukes them, telling them it is not for them to know the day nor the hour of such things.

Instead, the power that Jesus is speaking of will enable them to be His witnesses in the very city they are in, the nearby regions (of Judea and Samaria) and indeed, to the very ends of the Earth.

We carry on the mission they these Eleven began. We too receive the gift and power of the Holy Spirit that we might succeed.

In conclusion, let me remind you of the key elements we have learned about the Great Commission.

- We must go, prayerfully and wisely, but progress nonetheless
- We are to make disciples, committed followers and students of Christ
- We are to baptise in the name of the Father, Son and Holy Spirit
- We are to teach obedience to all that Jesus commanded
- We are to go in the power of the Holy Spirit

This task is too great for any one of us to complete on our own. With a whole lot of prayer, working with the united church, and in God's strength, we can do what has been asked of us.

Let us not forget the authority with which Jesus gave us these commands. They are not optional, not for anyone seeking to fully serve God. He has commanded it, so we will do it.

Fulfilling this Great Commission may take the rest of our lives. It may take us to far off places. It may mean stepping out of our comfort zones and doing things we would never have expected. It may cost us money, friends or even our lives.

We do it all for the One who loves us. We do it for the One who made all things, yet thought it not beneath Him to become human, and suffer and die for each of us.

We are His witnesses. We are His children. We are His servants. And we are His friends. Look to us, His church, and we will point you to Him – to Jesus.

He has saved my life. And I did not even know it needed saving. I go, with Bible in hand (and in heart), and I follow His lead -wherever it may take me. I urge you to join me.

What will you do?

My final set of questions for you to think about?

- Has this book encouraged you to want to fulfil the Great Commission?
- If someone asked you to explain the Great Commission to them now, how would you summarise it?
- What will you do now?

ABOUT THE AUTHOR

Andy was born in Essex, United Kingdom and came to faith at the age of fifteen. In the years that followed, he has developed a deep love for the Bible and served in church leadership in his local fellowships.

Andy is married to a wonderful wife, and is the father of four beautiful daughters.

The best place to find out more about Andy is at his website:

www.andy-brown.org

On the site, you will find blog posts and audio teachings. Subscribe to the blog to receive regular articles and also news about Andy's teaching and books.

You can find Andy's other book "A Journey with Jesus" on Amazon. It is a 40-day devotional, ideally suited to Lent, but can be read any time.

A JOURNEY WITH JESUS

40 Day Devotional

Andy Brown

Printed in Great Britain
by Amazon